# THE BOURNEMOUTH SYMPHONY ORCHESTRA

*Following page*
Sir Dan Godfrey (1868-1939),
founder of the Bournemouth Municipal Orchestra.

1893–1993

# THE BOURNEMOUTH SYMPHONY ORCHESTRA

*A Centenary Celebration*

SEAN STREET & RAY CARPENTER

THE DOVECOTE PRESS

First published in 1993 by The Dovecote Press Ltd.
Stanbridge, Wimborne, Dorset BH21 4JD

ISBN 1 874336 10 5

© Sean Street and Ray Carpenter 1993

Photoset in Sabon by
The Typesetting Bureau, Wimborne, Dorset
Printed and bound in Great Britain by
Biddles Ltd, Guildford and King's Lynn

# Contents

# *Foreword*

SIR MICHAEL TIPPETT OM
*President Emeritus, Bournemouth Orchestras*

Only a few years older than myself, its President Emeritus, the Bournemouth Symphony Orchestra can look back on a history of outstanding achievements and even wider acclaim. None of that has been accomplished without periods of struggle and misfortune. But all the major musicians I know who have been associated with the Bournemouth Orchestra have felt it to be an enterprise worth defending.

I myself take pride in the Bournemouth Symphony Orchestra for a variety of reasons. Its standards of execution have risen enormously. Provincial audiences can be assured of top-quality music-making and those in the metropolis will recognise something unique. The repertoire of the Orchestra is also challenging and imaginative, giving evidence of a commitment to music as a living art. Benefitting personally from this as a composer, I should say that it has been a particular privilege to hear the BSO interpret my works; and my composer-colleagues would undoubtedly share my enthusiasm for their skill and application in performing the music of the present-day. Lastly, the Orchestra exists as a community of warm-hearted individuals, and such cohesiveness comes across in their playing.

I am especially pleased that the BSO can look forward now to a future enlivened by tours, broadcasts and recordings, all of which confirm and reinforce the value placed upon them by sponsors and subscribers to their local concerts. In my own judgement, the BSO has now become a glorious, indispensable national treasure and I offer all my best wishes for their next 100 years.

*Michael Tippett*

# *Acknowledgements*

Without the help and co-operation of a number of individuals and organisations, this book could not have come to fruition. The support and advice of the management and musicians of the Bournemouth Orchestras has been of course crucial. We would like to thank Sir Michael Tippett O.M. for writing his Foreword, and Nigel Beale, Anthony Woodcock, Dion Butterworth and James Pestell of the Bournemouth Orchestras for practical guidance, friendly encouragement and help with pictures along the way. Our sincere thanks are also due the *Bournemouth Evening Echo*, and especially the hard working and patient staff of the paper's photographic library. We acknowledge permission to reproduce photographs of the Orchestra and Bournemouth from this collection. We are grateful to the staff of the Lansdowne Reference Library, Bournemouth for help with picture research and for permission to reproduce certain illustrations, notably The Square in 1923, the Souvenir of the 1000th concert and the Winter Gardens during one of Schwarz's 1947 concerts. Thanks also to the staff of Poole Museums and Simon Olding of the Russell-Cotes Art Gallery and Museum for their help. We acknowledge with gratitude permission to reproduce pictures of Bournemouth Square in 1900 and the 1920s from the collection of the Bournemouth Passenger Transport Association Ltd. We thank in particular Mr Vyvyan Jeffery for his invaluable help in the dating of certain pictures. John Gilbride took the cover photograph, as well as the reproduction of the Henry Lamb portrait of Godfrey, collected memorabilia and pictures of Andrew Litton and Brendan O'Brien. He also captured the Orchestra backstage, on the steps of Southampton Guildhall, during rehearsal and taking part in educational workshops. Donald Shepherd gave valuable help, information and pictures relating to the Bournemouth Symphony Chorus, and John Moreland supplied useful facts relating to the more recent history of the Orchestra, and in particular the work of The Friends. Kit Townend took the picture of the Chorus in rehearsal, and Bob Richardson that of the Bournemouth Symphony Orchestra and Dorset Youth Orchestra at the Poole Proms. Roger Hopkins donated

*Opposite page top:* Cranborne
Gardens, 1867  This rare early
photograph shows the site of The
Winter Gardens ten years before
the first building was erected.
The gardens had once been a
favourite spot of Lewis
Tregonwell, the founder of
Bournemouth, whose home, now
the Royal Exeter Hotel, stood at
the foot of the slope.

*Opposite page bottom:* The
Winter Gardens. Opened in 1877,
the original building, constructed
of glass and steel, was typical of
its era. Erected in Cranborne
Gardens, in its early days, the
Winter Gardens was used mainly
as an exhibition centre.

his expertise in the copying of certain rare pictures, and Stephen
Lloyd has been kind and generous in his support in the clarification
of certain points. We must also thank Wally Driffield, Geoffrey
Godfrey, John Myers, Bob Walker and Mike Chesters for pictures
and memorabilia. Other sources are as follows: the portrait of
Richard Austin was taken by Angus McBean, the photograph of
Percy Whitlock was supplied by the Whitlock Society, and Rudolf
Schwarz conducting, by E'don Photography. The photographs of the
exterior of the new Winter Gardens and the Queen at Poole Arts
Centre are by Kitchenham, and Gamba by E. A. White. Arthur
Coleman took the photograph of the Choir in 1951, the Kemsly
Studio took two pictures of Charles Groves, while the Press Associa-
tion supplied the picture of Groves and the Orchestra at the Royal
Festival Hall. George Hurst and Radu Lupu is a Bristol Evening Post
picture, and Tamas Vasary was photographed by Martin Hill. Suzie
E. Maider was responsible for the picture of Ronald Thomas and the
Sinfonietta, and the photograph of Norman Del Mar was sup-
plied by the Clarion Concert Agency Ltd. In any work of this
nature, it is important to recognise the work of previous research-
ers; Dan Godfrey's autobiography, *Memories and Music*, Geoffrey
Miller's 1970 book, *The Bournemouth Symphony Orchestra*, David
S. Young's *The Story of Bournemouth* as well as valuable works of
local history by Elizabeth Edwards and David and Rita Popham are
all publications with which the student of Bournemouth and its
Orchestra should be familiar. If we have omitted to thank or
acknowledge anyone who has contributed to this centenary tribute,
we apologise.

SEAN STREET AND RAYMOND CARPENTER, MAY, 1993

# Birth of an Orchestra

Poster for a Concert by the Italian Band, September 1882. The concerts were given in the Town Hall, at that time in a building situated where the Criterion Arcade now stands. The programme on this occasion included some Schumann and a liberal sprinkling of operatic gems.

Although we can trace the birth of the Bournemouth Municipal – later the Bournemouth Symphony Orchestra – to an exact date in May, 1893, it is important to give credit to the fact that Municipal music-making existed in the Town well before that date. As early as 1876, Bournemouth was served by the Italian Band, which had come to the area after working in Bath. There were sixteen players, and all had served in the Italian army, wore the appropriate uniform, and were supported by public subscription.

The late nineteenth century was a time of great development in Bournemouth. The Town was still very young; as recently as 1809 the only public building on a bleak heathland near the mouth of the little river Bourne was a wayside inn, the Tapps Arms. A year later, a Dorset Squire called Lewis Tregonwell drove through the area to explore its wild beauty. He and his wife fell in love with the place, and determined to build a summer residence for themselves there, now the Royal Exeter Hotel. Pines were planted and the air grew heavy with their scent as the years passed, and fashionable society followed Tregonwell's lead.

By the 1880's the population was nearing 20,000, a consciously shaped health resort formed under the eye of the architect Benjamin Ferry. Churches such as St Clement's, St Michael's and St Swithun's were built; some of the great residential roads grew up behind the East Cliff, and many celebrities and society notables made their homes among the pines, including the legendary Jersey Lily, Lily Langtry and Percy Florence Shelley, son of the poet. They were typical of the elegant and wealthy who brought a fashionable element of the dilettante to the growing town, and it was for them – and for the invalids resting among Bournemouth's fragrant walks and gardens, that the Italian Band played.

It was an island of manufactured elegance in an ancient countryside. In 1891, when Thomas Hardy published his novel, *Tess of the D'Urbervilles* he was referring to it as "Sandbourne"; "This fashionable watering-place ... was like a fairy place suddenly created by the stroke of a wand, and allowed to get a little dusty."

10

Then in 1892 came the first Corporation Military Band, formed by Signor E. Bertini and consisting of twenty one musicians; the band performed twice daily on the pier, and their popularity served to demonstrate to the authorities that greater things could be achieved in civic music-making.

So it was that Bournemouth set itself up for a unique experiment: a full municipal orchestra. To conduct and run this orchestra, the Council cast about among various possible names, finally settling on the son of one of the most famous bandsmen of the day, Dan Godfrey. Dan Godfrey Snr. was a nineteenth century legend, a name known to everyone even slightly interested in British Victorian music making. It was he whom the committee, charged with finding a musical director, first chose, but he was unavailable. As fate would have it, Godfrey Snr. was tardy at answering his mail, and the letter of invitation lay on his desk long enough for his son – another Dan Godfrey – to read it.

The younger Dan had recently returned from South Africa where he had been musical director of a touring opera company. He was not yet twenty five, had recently married a South African girl, and was looking for new fields to conquer. He was welcomed by the Committee on the day of his interview, and afterwards he lunched with the Mayor, Henry Newlyn at the Royal Exeter Hotel (Newlyn had formerly been proprietor there). Godfrey was to remember that

The Italian Band in Uniform. In 1876 a group of sixteen musicians from the Italian Army became the first publicly supported town band in Bournemouth. They were led by a Signor Bertini, and they were later to form the basis of the first Corporation Military Band.

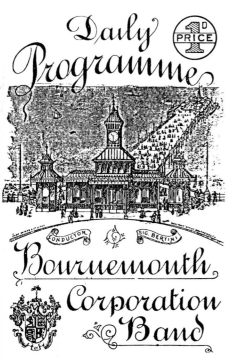

lunch for the rest of his life:

"I shall never forget the gorgeous Christchurch salmon, a dish fit for the "gods". It was fresh from the River Avon, crimped and served in a manner that would have satisfied the most fastidious epicure."

Godfrey Jnr. got the job, and started with a contract of £95 a week to run a band of thirty musicians, clothe them in an appropriate uniform, and obtain the music they were to play. The schedule was a heavy one – to play three times a day from Whitsun to October, although Dan was able to keep some time free for other projects by writing into the contract that his own conducting would involve him in only two concerts a week. Godfrey from the outset showed himself to be a shrewd man and a just inheritor of his famous father's mantle. Perhaps one of his most remarkable judgements in

*Left:* Programme, Bournemouth Corporation Band. An 1892 programme, with the band still under the baton of Signior Bertini, who also composed one of the items, a Mazurka entitled "It is Quite a Little Thing."

*Below:* Looking towards The Square from Invalids Walk in about 1900.

*Above:* Typical transport for the man-about-Bournemouth in the late nineteenth century. The donkey waits as patiently as the driver in this charming picture that shows something of the peaceful leafy ambience of the town at this time.

*Right:* Cartoon of Dan Godfrey Snr from *Vanity Fair*. The Godfrey family had dominated music making in the British Army from before the time of Waterloo. Dan Godfrey Senior had been appointed as bandmaster to the Grenadier Guards at the age of thirty, and took his band to play before Queen Victoria, as well as on tour to the United States.

the recruitment of the new band was to ensure that a large number of the musicians could double on both string and other instruments; thus this was both a military-style band and the foundation of something quite different . . . a full symphony orchestra.

The home for this bold new venture was a great glass pavilion built on high ground near the former home of the founder of Bournemouth, Lewis Tregonwell. It was called The Winter Gardens, and bore a striking resemblance to the glass houses at Kew Gardens. It had been built in 1877 as a multi-purpose exhibition and leisure hall, but it had never prospered. Now it was decided to turn the place into a "temple of music", a permanent home for Dan Godfrey's band.

The first concert in the Winter Gardens Pavilion was on the morn-

*Above:* Bournemouth Corporation Band. A young Dan Godfrey sits surrounded by the blue and gold uniforms and pill-box hats of the band that played first at the old Winter Gardens on Whit Monday, May 22nd 1893. A contemporary report said: "It seems as if the new band will 'catch on'; expressions of approval were heard on all hands, and a thorough success, as the conductor himself believes, is anticipated. A new and natty uniform has been provided which looks like a glorified smoking jacket, worked with thin gold braid, and turned at the collar and cuffs with red. The coats look warm and comfortable, and may we say it? 'chic'."

*Right:* "The Hot House". The leafy aisles of the Winter Gardens.

14

ing of May 22nd 1893, with an evening performance on the same day. Local interest was enormous, with 10,000 people coming to hear the music; the evening event was so well attended that the building became overcrowded, "packed so closely that locomotion was difficult." In spite of some doubting voices, the whole thing was a huge success, a triumph maintained through that first summer, the band playing three times a day, and Godfrey cleverly mixing popular and serious music in varied programmes to appeal to all tastes.

In September 1893, the Band of H.M. Grenadier Guards was engaged under the conductorship of Dan Godfrey Snr. to give two concerts at the Winter Gardens. After the concerts, the father stayed on to hear his son conduct, much to Dan Jnr's. trepidation. He need not have worried; the double event was a huge success, his father was delighted, and his public comments of praise undoubtedly did much to secure support from both audience and council alike.

So things continued through the early years; in 1895 a series of forty symphony concerts was inaugurated, and that figure later rose to sixty a year, the beginning of a Thursday evening concert tradition that was to establish itself as a part of the Town's cultural life. During the previous year Godfrey had crossed a major hurdle when his post as musical director was made a permanent one, thus giving him the security to begin a tradition which was to make the orchestra nationally famous for decades – his support of living British music. Edward German came to conduct his own work, as did Parry, Coleridge-Taylor, Stanford and Bantock. There were other great names too: Adelina Patti gave one of only three British recitals in Bournemouth, due to Godfrey's persuasion, and Clara Butt was a regular visitor.

There was much of the entrepreneur in Dan Godfrey, and it showed itself to good effect when in 1896 he was appointed as general manager of the Winter Gardens Pavilion, to give it its full title. Thus he ran not only the orchestra, but a whole range of concert parties, recitals, lectures and other more popular shows throughout the year. Within the last three years of the century he turned a loss of £961 round to a modest profit of £198. The variety of work that he instigated at the Winter Gardens may be judged from a review of the last concert held there in the nineteenth century, printed in *The Bournemouth Visitors' Directory*, January 2nd, 1901:

"The 25th of the present series of symphony concerts was given at the Winter Gardens on Monday afternoon and attracted a fairly large audience, who greatly enjoyed the excellent programme placed before them by Mr. Godfrey. One novelty was included, – the 'Walpurgisnacht' overture by Mendelssohn. Mr. Jos. Zeelander gave an adequate rendering of Lindner's very effective concerto for the

The Winter Gardens Stage. The stage is set for a performance by the Municipal Orchestra. The building was far from ideal as a concert hall. When it rained, the sound on the glass roof was so loud it was said to drown all but the most forte passages of the music. The musicians gave the place several uncomplimentary names, including "The Glass- house", "The Greenhouse" and "The Cucumber Frame." Note the potted palms on stage; *Punch* magazine declared: "The orchestral performers appear as it were planted amidst ferns."

'cello, a work which he has played before, and the symphony was Borodin's No. 2 in B Minor, a remarkably constructed composition which Mr Godfrey introduced some two seasons ago. For the rest we had three Slavonic dances by Dvorak (Book 1), and two melodies for strings by Grieg."

As the nineteenth century neared its end, the glass Winter Gardens had begun to acquire some rude nick-names from the musicians who regularly played there. Among these were The Hothouse, the Greenhouse and the Cucumber Frame. It was certainly not an ideal place to make music – let alone musical history – with strange acoustics and potted plants threatening to engulf the players by their very profusion. But the quality of the music-making that went on there was beyond question. In 1901, *The Musical Times* wrote:

"We have a strong suspicion that Mr Godfrey would have had no chance whatever of doing in a big manufacturing city or near London, what he has been allowed to do in the quietude of Bournemouth; and this, while taking duly into account the hardheaded progressiveness of a clever musician. At Bournemouth he has found a corporation wise enough to know what supports the prestige of the town . . ."

First British performances of major works, such as Borodin's Ballet music from Prince Igor and Bruch's Second Symphony gave the Town – and the Orchestra – a reputation far beyond its boundaries. Sir Alexander Mackenzie said that "Bournemouth is the first place to show any public spirit towards British music."

The original caption to this 1890's postcard reads "Dan Godfrey's Band at Bournemouth". By this time, the Orchestra had forsaken the uniforms for the more traditional formal concert dress. Later the poet, Christopher Hassall looked back with affectionate humour:

"Oh, pioneers of the stalwart brass
That shook the Tennysonian glass!
See them, salute them as they sat
In breeches blue and pill-box hat,
Puffing amid the potted palms
The less exacting bits of Brahms..."

# The New Century

In 1914 the Bournemouth Natural Science Society published its *Natural History of Bournemouth and District*, in which the town's virtues were extolled in every possible field imaginable, from its topography to its sewage system. We are reminded that:

"Bournemouth can fairly claim to be an ideal town. It is bountifully endowed by Nature, is situated in practically the centre of the southern coast, and is sheltered by the higher lands and the various belts of pine trees from the colder winds of the north and east. The rapidity of the town's growth has been phenomenal; in sixty years the population has increased from 695 to 80,000."

May 1914 saw the coming of age of the Bournemouth Municipal Orchestra, and Dan Godfrey proudly announced the fact, adding that in so doing the town had created "a record unprecedented in the history of municipal music making in this country." And through the first fourteen years of the new century the cavalcade of English

The Municipal Orchestra, Godfrey at the Podium.

M. J. R., B. No. 283

music continued, and Dan was justified in claiming that "There is hardly a British composer of note who has not appeared as conductor of his own works. To give a brief idea of the scope of the concerts, it might be mentioned that 135 British composers have contributed 454 separate works. Many of the compositions have obtained at these concerts their first actual performances."

Gustav Holst once cycled from London to Bournemouth with a new score, arriving before the conductor was up, only to be mistaken for the paper boy by Godfrey's wife, who called down to him to "Put the papers in the service lift"; shortly after that, Holst walked in on the drowsy Godfrey, and threw the score on the bed adding "Please sir, I've brought the papers". In addition to Holst, Vaughan Williams came to hear Godfrey interpret some of his early music, and Rutland Boughton, whose greatest fame was to rest on his phenomenally successful opera, "The Immortal Hour" conducted works. Landon Ronald conducted, as did Hamilton Harty, who gave the first performance of his Irish Symphony. Ethel Smyth conducted her overture, "The Wreckers", and in 1908, the greatest prize of all, Edward Elgar who conducted a full concert of his work on the Winter Gardens stage. In 1910 Fritz Kreisler gave only the second performance of the Elgar Violin Concerto just over a week after its London premiere.

In that same year, Bournemouth celebrated the centenary of its founding by Lewis Tregonwell with a ten day fête, with varied entertainments. There were confetti battles and carnivals, and an international aviation meeting at Southbourne, where a shadow was thrown over events by the first fatal accident involving a British

The Square, from Old Christchurch Road, in 1904.

*Above:* Edwardian Bournemouth, from the Pier.

*Right:* Famous names from the percussion section of the orchestra, 1908. W.W. Bennett Junior and Senior between them were members of the percussion section from the birth of the orchestra to 1948. Both men specialised in xylophone solos at the more popular concerts, as did another legendary figure, Billy Byrne.

pilot, the Hon. Charles Stewart Rolls. To mark the Centenary, Godfrey gave a spectacular concert, in which he shared the podium with Elgar, German, Mackenzie, Parry and Stanford. The following year came an honour that he must have savoured dearly, when the BMO was invited to give a concert of British music at the Festival of Empire in London's Crystal Palace, after which he was welcomed and celebrated at a dinner attended by most of the great contemporary names in music. It was the first time the orchestra had played in London, and it was one of its greatest triumphs. The Times wrote of the occasion:

"Mr Godfrey has succeeded in making the public take a genuine interest in British music and those who make it. That a town like Bournemouth should become one of the most important musical centres of England is a curious commentary on our way of doing things. . ."

In the same year, another landmark was reached when the Bournemouth Municipal Choir was formed. By the start of the First World War this had grown to 250 members, and had performed with the Orchestra many times, including notable performances of "Elijah" by Mendelssohn, "Blest Pair of Sirens" by Parry, "The Messiah" by Handel and "Merrie England" under its composer, Edward German.

The Fairlight Glen Tram Disaster, May 1st, 1908. Trams had been running in Bournemouth since 1902, and this was the first tram accident in Britain. The brakes went out of control as it came down the hill from Poole towards The Square. It plunged into Fairlight Glen (Part of the Upper Gardens) at about 75 m.p.h. The death toll was seven, with twenty six injured.

Municipal Orchestra Programme, 1909. Some programmes carried the words: "The Scent of the Pines – The Celebrated Bournemouth Perfume."

*Opposite page:* Two Edwardian views of Bournemouth Station. In one, the London train has just arrived at a station that still retains intact the structure its Victorian builders intended. The importance of the railway to Bournemouth was crucial to its development as a resort. It also was a vital link for the Orchestra with the rest of the country, and in particular, London.

The first Chorus Master was Dr. H. Holloway and the accompanist was Alice Harding. H. Arthur Kettle was Hon. Secretary.

At the opening of the 21st season, the Orchestra and Choir joined together to perform "Faust" by Berlioz. The concert was acclaimed, and was proudly recalled in a commemorative book celebrating the coming of age, and stating that it was "one of the most successful choral concerts on local record. The exacting nature of the music by Berlioz is well known, and the adequate performance by both chorus and orchestra attracted large audiences and set the standard for further developments on similar lines." But municipal musical life was as much about hard work as it was about glamour and acclamation. And certainly the Bournemouth musicians worked hard. As Dan Godfrey wrote in 1914:

22

23

A musician's-eye-view of Dan Godfrey, seen from the Principal 'Cello's seat!

The Arcade, 1910, decked out for the Centenary Fetes. At the Gervis Place end was (and still is) a balcony, where musicians would play for visitors and shoppers.

"During the summer season, from May till October, the Municipal Orchestra plays each morning on Bournemouth Pier, and each evening at the Winter Gardens, assisted by popular entertainers and vocalists. On Wednesday afternoons a Symphony Concert is given at the Winter Gardens, and on the other afternoons the band is divided into sections for the Pier performances . . . During the winter months the mornings are devoted to rehearsals, and there are afternoon and evening concerts at the Winter Gardens from October to May."

In addition to the Orchestra, the Corporation still maintained a Military band of twenty five players, performing every morning except Sunday all the year round in the Central Pleasure Gardens. On summer afternoons it played in the various other pleasure gardens of the borough, and in the evenings on Bournemouth or Boscombe Pier.

The Town's musical director was justly proud of what he had achieved in twenty one years:

"Bournemouth possesses an absolutely unique record in its enterprise for music. Not only does it maintain the most complete permanent Municipal Orchestra in the world, but does so without a charge on the rates, the Winter Gardens being now self-supporting."

Much of this success grew out of the urbane and artistically sympathetic Mayoralty of Dr. H. S. McCalmont Hill, whom Godfrey called "One of the most lovable personalities in the municipal life

of Bournemouth." He showed strong support for any scheme that aimed at the development of municipal music, and there is no doubt that Dan found in him a strong ally. The two men had much in common, not least their delight in progress and innovation. In 1914 McCalmont Hill was able to look at the huge expansion of the town and publicly demonstrate his belief that in the "newness" of Bournemouth lay its greatest opportunities:

"Bournemouth is a town unhampered by a past. There are many English cities royal, walled, ancient, which find it difficult to adapt themselves to the exigences of modern life ... There should be no new setting for ancient jewels. Bournemouth grew and is still growing."

The Edwardian years were eventful ones in many ways, and Dan Godfrey found himself tested diplomatically at times outside the course of civic duty; in 1907, the Kaiser visited Highcliffe Castle and offered the services of his band to play at the Winter Gardens. The intrepid Bournemouth music master made an uncomfortable trip to the German Emperor's yacht, "Hohenzollern" "in a closed pinnace tossed about by a choppy sea." In return for the favour, the then Mayor of Bournemouth, Alderman Bridge called at Highcliffe Castle to offer the services of the Municipal Orchestra. However,

The Kings of British Music. In 1910, during the Centenary Fetes, some of the greatest British performers and composers came to Bournemouth. With Godfrey in this picture are (Standing) – Sir Edward German and Sir Hubert Parry. (Seated) – Sir Edward Elgar, Sir Alexander Mackenzie and Sir Charles Stanford. It is no coincidence that Elgar and Stanford sit as far apart as possible. They had a strong and mutual antipathy.

25

The orchestra of the German Emperor's yacht, *Hohenzollern* with Dan Godfrey, during their visit to Bournemouth in 1907. In his memoirs, Godfrey tells this story: "During one of the Emperor's visits to Norway, his officers were forbidden to cycle on board. This order was disobeyed, and the offender was reprimanded by the Kaiser in such an insulting manner that the indignant officer struck him. For this impetuous action he was condemned to death, a sentence which was, however, not carried out. But later he was taken to a precipice and allowed to ride over, and the news was circulated that he had committed suicide."

Souvenir photograph of the 1000th Symphony Concert, January 25th, 1912. Underneath it was written, , "With Mr Dan Godfrey's Compliments."

as Godfrey was later to explain in his memoirs "he was most un-
ceremoniously treated, and was not granted the courtesy of an interview."

A happier musical encounter had occurred in 1903 when the
Princess Louise, the Duchess of Argyle, accompanied by the Duke of
Argyle and the Earl and Countess of Malmesbury attended a Winter
Gardens concert. The programme began with two pieces by Elgar,
and ended with "Songs Without Words" by Mendelssohn and
"Whistling Rufus", "the last two items played by special desire of
the Princess." At the same concert the Countess of Malmesbury
played a violin solo.

But now the War clouds were looming, and things would never be
quite the same again.

The Pier Approach in about 1912.

# The Great War and After

In May 1914, Bournemouth saw its first motor buses, working alongside the trams. As the world moved into war, life in the town continued much as it had always done – at least on the surface. The orchestra still played, and the river of British music flowed on, including the first out-of-town performance of Vaughan Williams' London Symphony. Also in that same 1914/15 season were a number of performances of Rutland Boughton's famous work "The Immortal Hour".

Audiences declined during the war years due as much as anything to the difficulty of finding a way through the rhododendrons and pines in the blackout, but the music-making continued triumphantly. Once during a concert, a large explosion was heard nearby; it was an anxious moment, and some of the audience feared a German attack; however, it turned out to be a mine that had washed up on the

Trams and cars in The Square in about 1922. The original circular island was converted to an oblong shape to accomodate the tram tracks. Shortly after this time a passenger shelter was erected in the middle of The Square.

beach, and was being detonated. Little else touched the town until news of the universal casualties began to reach Bournemouth too. George Butterworth, the young English composer who died in the war, was honoured by a performance of his "A Shropshire Lad" Rhapsody, and Ethel Smyth returned – now notorious as a suffragette with a spell in prison behind her – to conduct more of her music. It would not be long before she was to play a crucial role in the preservation of the orchestra. Shortly before the Armistice, Parry died, and his life was celebrated by a performance of his "Symphonic Variations", a work he had himself first conducted in Bournemouth in 1901.

Just before the end of hostilities the orchestra celebrated its twenty-fifth anniversary. True to form, British music was well represented, with Stanford and Edward German both conducting their own works. In 1921 Sibelius came to conduct his music, and in the same year Arnold Bax sat in the audience as the BMO gave the world premiere performance of his tone poem "Tintagel".

There were two memorable Elgar nights: one when the great man himself returned to conduct the E Flat Symphony, and the other when a 'Cellist called Barbirolli played his 'Cello Concerto; this young man was later to become better known as a conductor . . . Sir John Barbirolli. History was being made during every season.

Female Emancipation, or simply wartime necessity? The Amateur String Orchestra, in 1919, with their conductor, probably Bertram Lewis, who was also principal first violin with the BMO.

*Above:* A light hearted moment during rehearsals for the first Easter Festival in 1922.

*Right:* Letter from Adrian Boult to Dan Godfrey, congratulating him on his knighthood. The letter is interesting, in that it recognises Ethel Smyth's role in the affair.

KENSINGTON 1747.

6, CHELSEA COURT,
S.W.3.

6th June 1922.

Dear Sir. Dan Godfrey.

        May I send you very hearty congratulations on the well
deserved honour that has come to you.    I was so very interested
to see the article in the Sphere recently, because I had so often
heard Francis and Geoffrey Toye say how much they owed to your
concerts in their young days.        I am sorry that I have not
had that privilege also, but my parents have now come to live not
more than 25 miles from Bournemouth, and as I am an inveterate
bicyclist I want to come over sometimes to hear you.    Perhaps
you will be so good as to send me your next season's particulars
when they are out.

        Dame Ethel Smyth will be rejoicing I know, because
it was owing to her intervention that many of us have written
to the Prime Minister to urge him to  take this very excellent
step.

                                        from my very sincerely

                                        Adrian C.B.Boult.

Sir Dan Godfrey,
        Winter Gardens, Bournemouth.

30

In the Spring of 1922 the BMO began a series of annual Easter Festivals, in which the tradition of British music was to be upheld in an even more spectacular way. The first Festival lasted five weeks, with more than a dozen British Composers conducting their own works, including Ethel Smyth, Elgar, Edward German, Granville Bantock, Gustav Holst, Vaughan Williams, Henry Wood and Eugene Goosens. Godfrey later declared triumphantly "The five weeks' festival was a financial success . . . Naturally the first object of our festival was to induce visitors to make a prolonged stay in Bournemouth at Easter, and this was accomplished most successfully, but from an art point of view it has been generally acknowledged that a valuable service has been done to British music by the performance of so many works of importance."

Then as if to cap it all, a campaign led by Ethel Smyth to gain Godfrey the recognition he deserved nationally came to fruition,

Festival Guests of 1922. Godfrey stands in the grounds of the Winter Gardens behind Sir Alexander Mackenzie, Dame Ethel Smyth, Sir Henry Wood and Sir Edward German, all of whom conducted the BMO during the Festival.

31

Sir Dan Godfrey with the
Municipal Orchestra, shortly
after his knighthood. The set –
wherever it is – looks somewhat
precarious!

when the Prime Minister, Lloyd George, recommended Godfrey for
a knighthood. On June 3rd it was announced as part of the birthday
honours . . . "For valuable services to British music."

"We are going forward in Bournemouth", said Godfrey, and
indeed it appeared that for once all the omens were favourable; plans
were in hand to build a giant new theatre and concert hall on the
other side of the Pleasure Gardens to replace the ageing "Cucumber
Frame", the Easter Festivals were set to become an annual event, and
the list of musical successes grew ever longer. Arthur Bliss conducted
his new "Colour Symphony", the first performance of Sibelius' Fifth
Symphony in Bournemouth was given, and Hamilton Harty conducted his Piano Concerto for the first time. And the Easter Festival
of 1923 – when it came – proved even more adventurous, with 22
British composers conducting their own works, including some who
were to become enduring popular favourites, among them Albert
Ketelbey and Eric Coates.

1923 also saw major developments elsewhere that were to have a
profound effect on the orchestra's reputation. In a year which saw
the first cup final at Wembley, Noel Coward's plays, *The Vortex* and
the controversial *Fallen Angels* and Baldwin succeed Bonar Law as
Prime Minister, the British Broadcasting Company opened its eighth
radio station – 6BM – in premises over a pram and cycle shop at 72,
Holdenhurst Road, with a transmitter backing onto the cemetery
in Bushey Road. The Mayor of Bournemouth, Alderman Charles
Cartwright, spoke at the opening. The presence of the radio station,

initially broadcasting only locally, but later to provide a link into the BBC's developing national network, was to mean regular broadcasts that would make the Municipal Orchestra respected and admired throughout Britain.

In the winter of 1923, Bartok played his "Rhapsody for Piano and Orchestra" with the BMO. The following year came another Easter celebration. Sir Henry Wood conducted Tchaikowsky's Fifth Symphony and Delius' "Brigg Fair", drawing a sympathetic review from a *Times* critic, who praised specific sections of the orchestra warmly:

"One must mention the first horn, who played the solo in the symphony extremely well, and the principal violin, Mr Bertram Lewis, who besides being an efficient pilot, played all solo passages with musical feeling. One's admiration for the two gentlemen (three in times of stress) who are responsible for at least ten percussion instruments, amounts almost to awe, when one thinks of the number of parts on which they have to keep an eye, apart from remembering where they have laid the tambourine, and where the hammers of the glockenspiel. Especially admirable is the playing of the timpanist, who has a capacity in his wrists for tone colour that many pianists might covet for their fingers."

1925 saw an Easter Festival with Rutland Boughton back with the

The Square in 1923, looking across to the gardens and Old Christchurch Road. The era of the Charabanc has well and truly arrived!

*Above:* The Bournemouth Municipal Orchestra outside the old Winter Gardens in 1926. A genial Godfrey (eighth from the left, front row) is flanked by his deputy conductor, Montague Birch on his left, and Orchestra Leader Bertram Lewis on his right. This was during one of the great Festivals which during the 1920's made Bournemouth a national centre for British music.

*Right:* Poster for the last Concerts in the old Winter Gardens. Ben Davies had sung with Godfrey's 1893 band. Another link with those early days came in the evening when "Ole Bill" (The Orchestra's original percussionist) played one of his famous xylophone solos. The baritone, Frank Phillips, married Sir Dan Godfrey's daughter. He later went on to become well known as a BBC radio announcer.

SATURDAY Afternoon and Evening (March 16th) at 3 and 7,

# SIR DAN GODFREY'S LAST ANNUAL CONCERTS

also the

FINAL PERFORMANCES of the MUNICIPAL ORCHESTRA in the WINTER GARDENS
1893-1929

The following distinguished and popular Artistes have kindly consented to appear:—

AFTERNOON at 3.

## SIR HAMILTON HARTY

will conduct his Poem " WITH THE WILD GEESE," and will play with JEAN GENNIN his IRISH RHAPSODY for Flute and Piano.

### Miss MARIE HALL
(THE RENOWNED VIOLINIST)

### Mr. BEN DAVIES
(THE WORLD-FAMOUS TENOR) who is shortly retiring

### The Rev. CANON MARSH, M.A.
will play Piano Solos

### Mr. FRANK PHILLIPS
(THE DISTINGUISHED BARITONE)

The MUNICIPAL ORCHESTRA - Conductor : Sir DAN GODFREY

Reserved Seats 7/6, 5/9, 4/9, 3/- and 2/4. Balcony 3/6. Unreserved Seats—Balcony 2/4, Annexe 1/6 (all including Tax) Annual Tickets and Coupons not available.

EVENING at 7.      Three hours' Entertainment.

THE BOURNEMOUTH GASWORKS BAND (Conductor: Mr. A. H. METCALF) will play from 7 to 7.45

### Miss MARIE HALL

### Mr. BEN DAVIES

MR. FRANK PHILLIPS
will sing Prologue to Pagliacci, etc.

MR. A. W. KETELBEY
will conduct some of his popular compositions.

BROMLEY CARTER
(Entertainer)

MIDDLETON WOODS
(Entertainer)

ERNEST WELLBELOVED
(The Popular Reciter)

"OLE BILL" (W. Byrne) will play a Xylophone Solo

THE BOURNEMOUTH LABOUR MALE VOICE CHOIR

THE MUNICIPAL ORCHESTRA - - Conductor: SIR DAN GODFREY

The Programme will include Popular Items Reminiscent of the past 36 years.

Reserved Seats 4/9, 3/6, 3/- and 2/4. Unreserved Seats—Balcony 1/10, Annexe 1/2 (all including Tax).

Annual Tickets and Coupons not available.

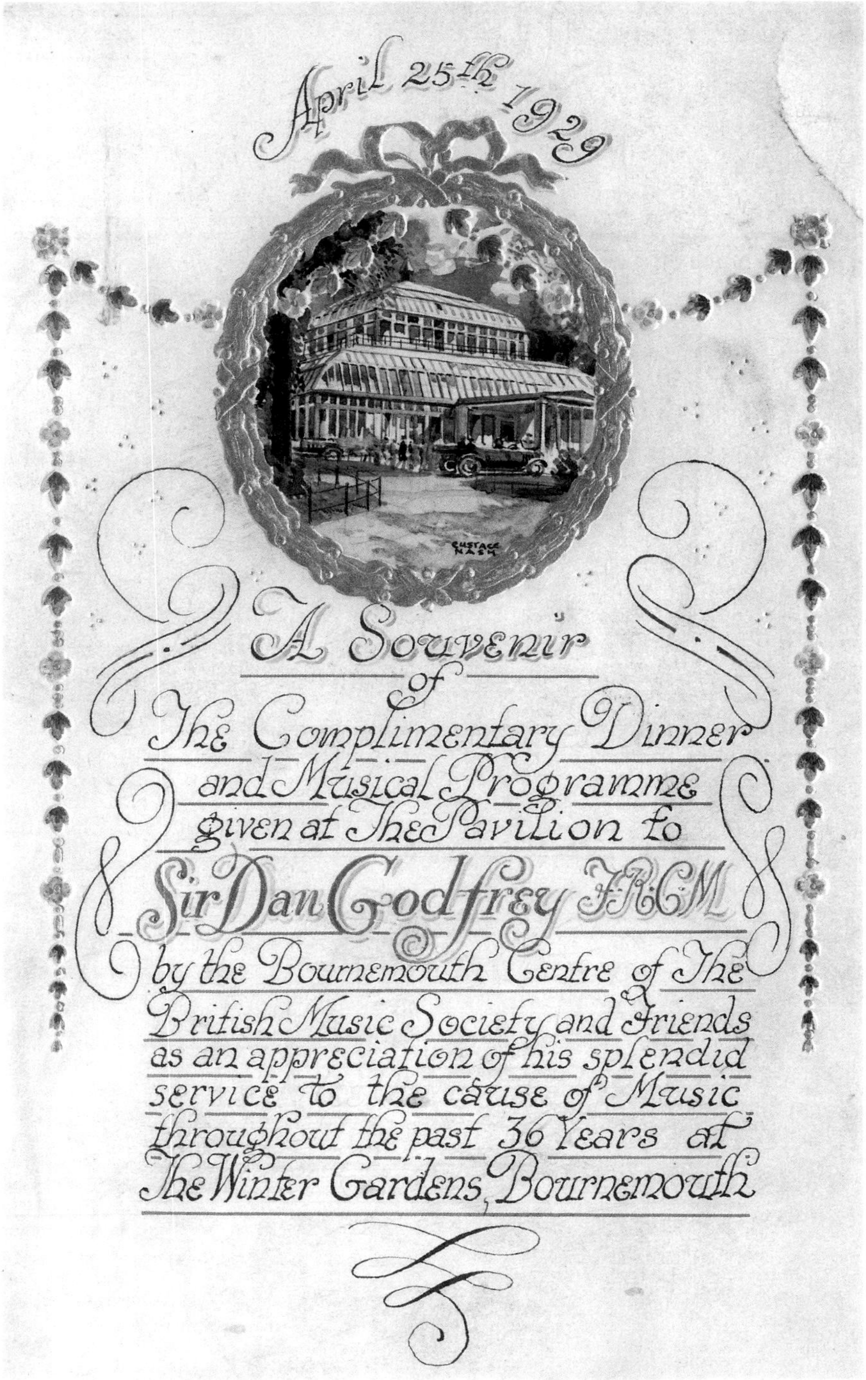
April 25th 1929
EUSTACE NASH
A Souvenir
of
The Complimentary Dinner
and Musical Programme
given at The Pavilion to
Sir Dan Godfrey F.R.C.M.
by the Bournemouth Centre of The
British Music Society and Friends
as an appreciation of his splendid
service to the cause of Music
throughout the past 36 Years at
The Winter Gardens, Bournemouth

Bournemouth acknowledges its debt: menu cover of a 1929 dinner in honour of Sir Dan Godfrey.

This photograph shows the Municipal Orchestra, Choir and soloists in the Winter Gardens, during the last days of the old Glass House. Bournemouth's first permanent choral society had been founded by Madame Cecil Newling. After her death in April 1911, the Bournemouth Municipal Choir was formed, numbering some 250 selected singers, to perform with the Orchestra. Godfrey was the first conductor. At first, the choir was the responsibility of Bournemouth Corporation, but became self-governing after the first World War, a status it retained until becoming part of the Western Orchestral Society in 1979.

Glastonbury Players (Boughton had attempted to establish a sort of English Bayreuth around his music at Glastonbury). This time he brought a number of his works, notably his operatic version of Thomas Hardy's play, "The Queen of Cornwall." It was a memorable occasion, and Hardy himself came over from his home, Max Gate, near Dorchester, to witness it.

By the 1926 Festival, with the new Pavilion theatre now started, and a place in it promised for the orchestra, the musical life of Bournemouth looked set for new challenges and triumphs. The Orchestra, in addition to its live concert work, was making many records, including a number of novelties featuring two well known flautists, Jean and Pierre Gennin. The earliest recordings of the Municipal Orchestra date from 1914, and include works by Saint-Saens, Grieg, German and Elgar. The late twenties saw a run of popular pieces – showing what the BMO had always been good at – mixing the light and the serious in music. Hence, in consecutive records, one can find Valse Triste by Sibelius and the Minuet from Act One of Don Giovanni by Mozart, followed by a piece called "Zip Zip" by a long term leader of the orchestra, Byron Brooke.

The orchestra played a very real role in the creation as well as the interpretation of these recorded pieces: also during the twenties the almost legendary percussionist W. Byrne composed what might almost have been the Bournemouth Orchestra's anthem – "Whispering Pines." In the meantime the old Winter Gardens was still home, and now the microphones of the BBC were often present to broadcast concerts. The last Easter Festival happened in 1928, and in the same year Godfrey conducted a concert version of Wagner's "Tannhauser" with the Orchestra and Municipal Choir. The following year saw the last regular concerts in the orchestra's birthplace before its ultimate demolition six years later in 1935, and the orchestra's move to the new Pavilion. At the last of all they played the Introduction to Act Three of Wagner's Lohengrin. A member of the audience on that night, Leslie Smith, later wrote:

"I can never hear this outstanding piece of music without being deeply moved and the occasion made it even more moving than usual. There is a peculiar, pleading plaintiveness and intensity about that trombone call, particularly as it reaches its climax, which never fails to bring a tear to my eye, and how much more so on this sad occasion of the passing of the old Palm House. . . . There was something about the old Palm House which could not be transported into any other concert hall."

# Highs and Lows

The Bournemouth Pavilion was opened on Tuesday, March 19th, 1929 by His Royal Highness, the Duke of Gloucester. It contained a theatre, a ballroom, three restaurants and two bars. From here nationally networked broadcasts spread the BMO's reputation far and wide. 6BM had ceased operating as a local station, but a continuing BBC presence in the town ensured that such events were fed into the new cross-country wireless transmissions. The Wednesday concerts were regularly featured, as were occasionally the Sunday evening performances. Thus it was on May 21st 1933 that Britain eavesdropped on the orchestra's fortieth anniversary concert from the Pavilion. For this the theatre was full to capacity, and the

On the Road. The Bournemouth Municipal Orchestra set off by Charabanc for an undisclosed destination in the early 1930's. Social life of the Orchestra used to include an annual outing with Godfrey.

38

The Pavilion Theatre,
Bournemouth.

orchestra had been augmented by a number of its original players from the first 1893 concert, notably the horn player William
Warren, and the bassist Pietro Bottiglieri. Sir Dan drew attention
to their presence from the podium, and speeches were made. In
charge of radio transmissions locally for the Bournemouth station
was Chief Engineer and Programme Representative, Bill Furse-Mills,
who recalled the furore within the BBC created by Sir Dan's words:

"After playing the Grand March, *Land of Hope and Glory* at the
conclusion of the concert, Sir Dan excelled himself by turning to the
audience – and the BBC microphones – and saying that he hoped all
the wireless listeners who had enjoyed the concert would come to
Bournemouth for their holidays!"

This was almost certainly the first and only broadcast advertise-
ment heard by British listeners until the advent of the commercial
radio stations in Normandy and Luxembourg. The next morning the
Director of Outside Broadcasts in London rang Bill Furse-Mills:

"He was very concerned about the possible contravention of the
BBC's licence which forbade any form of publicity in its programmes, and I had to warn Sir Dan that he was never to do it
again!"

Just over a year after this anniversary, on September 30th 1934,

Elder statesman of music. Although Dan Godfrey was due to retire after his sixty fifth birthday in March 1934, he actually stayed on as unofficial musical director throughout that Summer. This picture celebrates forty years in Bournemouth.

A more controversial view of Sir Dan, by Henry Lamb. Godfrey hated it, saying "I do not feel that one person in a hundred will like it, and I hope it will not be hung anywhere in public." In fact it disappeared from view for many years, until rediscovered by Raymond Carpenter in the Orchestra's music library at the Winter Gardens, wrapped in brown paper.

came an even more sentimental occasion, when Godfrey retired. Of all years for this champion of British music to go, as fate would have it, there could not have been a more poignant one than 1934, the year that Elgar, Delius and Holst all died. Godfrey had reached his sixty fifth birthday in the Spring, but had stayed on while a successor was found. This turned out to be Richard Austin; the thirty year old son of a well known musical father – Frederic Austin – was appointed after a series of concert auditions when the orchestra was conducted by a number of young hopefuls. It was a time of inevitable sadness and conflict; the past and the future were palpably meeting, and a number of Godfrey's ageing musicians were to leave with him.

There were emotional scenes at his farewell concert, witnessed by the nation on radio, when Godfrey broke down at the podium, and

Richard Austin. The man with the difficult task of taking up Godfrey's mantle; in fact he went on to develop music festivals for which the BMO was built up to a force of 75 players, making it the largest municipal orchestra in the world.

41

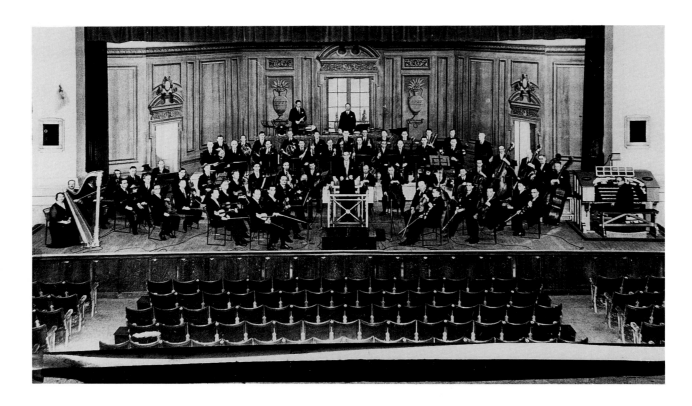

Richard Austin with the Orchestra in the Pavilion, Bournemouth, 1939. The Georgian "Stately home" set became a familiar backdrop to orchestral concerts at the Pavilion. Austin had been developing new audiences with Thursday afternoon concerts, but at the outbreak of war, shortly after this picture was taken, the Orchestra was reduced to 24 players, and Austin resigned. The leader is Harold Fairhurst, and seated at the organ is Percy Whitlock.

had to be assisted by Montague Birch, his deputy. But it had to be, and at the end of the concert – as everyone sang "Auld Lang Syne", Godfrey and Austin stood with arms linked, smiling. More than 2,000 concerts, over 800 works by British composers, with 160 composers conducting their own work . . . all in forty one years. It was a hard act to follow.

Austin's answer was to make the Sunday popular concerts more symphonic, and he even introduced a series of lecture recitals in local schools. Then, in only his second year, he brought back the idea of the Easter Musical Festivals, this time inviting some of the greatest contemporary names in conducting to take the podium; Boult came, so did Barbirolli and Beecham, and in 1936, at the second Festival Igor Stravinsky conducted "Pulcinella", "The Firebird" and his "Capriccio" for Piano and Orchestra, with his son as soloist.

Sir Dan Godfrey conducted again with the BMO – at least once a year at the Pavilion – and in November 1935, back in the old home of the Winter Gardens. It had been decided that the glass house was to be demolished, and a farewell concert was planned. Who but Godfrey could have conducted it? The 1812 Overture – a staple part of the Bournemouth diet since the earliest days – was on the bill, and the place was packed. They finished with Haydn's "Farewell" Symphony, at the end of which musicians one by one stop playing, blow out a candle and leave the platform. It was the sort of theatre Dan

Godfrey excelled at, and when at the end, he snuffed the last candle, and only the sound of the beating rain could be heard, the moment was loaded with significance. Within a month, the Winter Gardens had ceased to exist.

There is a symmetry about Godfrey's life and career in Bournemouth; a son had been born to him the day before his first appointment in 1893, and in the late twenties – like his father – was making music in South Africa. Then, in this poignant year of farewell, that same son – now forty one – died of a heart attack in Durban.

Meanwhile, in 1937, Austin saw Bournemouth's reputation grow again at his pleading, with strong help from Henry Wood, and the size of the orchestra grew to 61 players. The Pavilion was making money, the weekly broadcasts were a huge success, and Austin's star was in the ascendant.

Sir Dan lived on in Bournemouth and was presented with a controversial portrait of himself at a Richard Austin concert. The picture was hung in the Pavilion for a while much to Sir Dan's disgust (he hated it), but was subsequently removed. In 1939, following a brain spasm during a Pavilion rehearsal, he died on July 20th, and the funeral took place in St Peter's church during a raging thunderstorm.

Memories of the Maestro. On July 20th, 1939, Dan Godfrey died. In this collection – symbols of more than forty years' music-making in Bournemouth – the tambourine was signed by legendary names including Melba and Sibelius. Also in the picture, a manuscript of a Waltz by Godfrey's father, some batons and Godfrey's top hat, as well as a contract of 1893, family photos, a record, and – bridging time – an extract of a score by the Orchestra's latter-day President Emeritus, Sir Michael Tippett for his opera, "The New Moon."

Percy Whitlock. Seen here at the console of the Pavilion's famous Compton Organ, Percy Whitlock was a popular musical figure in the town, and was a major part of Montague Birch's wartime Sunday concerts. He was also a fine composer in his own right, and many of his works were played by the BMO.

Under Austin, the Orchestra and Municipal Choir flourished, and at the March Festival of 1939 the combined forces gave a fine performance of Brahms' "Requiem". Beecham conducted the Seventh Symphony of Beethoven, but with war in Europe looming, Rafael Kubelik was unable to get out of Czechosovakia to conduct the final concert of the week. It was a major achievement for Austin, but it was the climax before the collapse. The day after one of the Orchestra's September concerts, War finally came.

One more Festival was to come – in February 1940, when Felix Weingartner came to conduct Beethoven. Then, with the reduction of the orchestra to just 24 players, Austin resigned. Montague Birch picked up the pieces of what was left, and this handful continued to play for the popular market in the pit and on the bandstand. It might have looked as though serious music making in Bournemouth was dead, but this was far from the case. A new independent orchestra – The Wessex Philharmonic – was formed, based on a core of redundant musicians from the BMO. Throughout the war years, the Wessex Phil. played on around the area, although notably in St Peter's Hall in Hinton Road, just across the road from where the great

mentor of Bournemouth music had so recently been laid to rest.

Meanwhile Montague Birch struggled to keep the municipal flag flying with popular Sunday concerts. If ever music had a faithful, undemonstrative friend it was in the figure of "Monty" Birch, back row violinist, accompanist and deputy to two fine conductors, now he was in charge of this tiny group of musicians. Even so, at the height of war, he achieved an audience for popular Sunday concerts in the old Godfrey tradition, while the 40 strong Wessex Philharmonic played on in rather cramped conditions at St Peter's Hall, entertaining workers with lunchtime concerts. And some great names became associated with this scratch orchestra, including Sargent, Constant Lambert, Henry Wood and Basil Cameron. Austin himself came back to Bournemouth to conduct them twice, and the legendary 'cellist Beatrice Harrison played with them.

Service men and women came to Bournemouth, audiences swelled for both orchestras and incredibly under Birch's quiet guidance, the BMO actually went into profit. What the war had demonstrated – in a way no one could have predicted – was that music was alive and well in the town, and – more vitally – it had a future. In 1943 came

Bournemouth Municipal Musicians playing on the pier in 1939. The audience is sparse, and apparently not over-attentive. Members of the Orchestra played often on the Pier during the late 1930's as part of their duties as civic employees.

45

the fiftieth anniversary, with Adrian Boult and Montague Birch sharing the conducting at two concerts. On May 20th, the *Echo* took an appropriate look over its shoulder:

"' When the days are shortening, when the stormy s'wester shrieks, when the leaves are falling, when the flowers are few and sad, and after all the galaxy of summer beauty, we are left to comfort ourselves as best we may with chrysanthemums and Michaelmas daisies; when all nature is fast settling down to her long winter sleep, when all around speaks of death and decay, then music asserts her claims.'

"Those words were penned by a local music critic nearly fifty years ago, after he had attended a concert by the Bournemouth Municipal Orchestra, and though the season of the year is not the same, they are not inapt today, when, in the midst of the most terrible war the world has seen, music certainly has its claims as one of the people's greatest stand-bys and tonics.

"And the Municipal Orchestra, which on Sunday celebrates its fiftieth anniversary, holds a proud place in musical circles for the manner in which, year in and year out, it provides the people of Bournemouth with all that is best in music, sometimes in the face of very great wartime difficulties."

Those difficulties were exemplified on the very day of the anniversary, when the town received its worst air-raid of the war.

Under Birch during the early 1940's, the BMO continued its recording career with Decca, including works by Delibes – music from "Coppelia", Ponchielli – "The Dance of the Hours", and Schubert – the "Marche Militaire". In all seven records were made, all recorded in the Pavilion, and they are collectors' items today, although – with the orchestra in its run-down wartime state – they are not particularly distinguished either for their adventurous enterprise or their execution.

But gradually things improved; more players came, and full houses became the order of the day, with music of a symphonic scale once again ringing out from the Pavilion stage. It seemed that a corner had been turned; from 1944 onwards an air of optimism prevailed amongst music lovers in Bournemouth. Laurence Harker, manager of the Pavilion, drew up plans for an enlarged orchestra, based in its own home ... a concert hall that would double as a conference venue.

At first the latter part of the scheme fell on deaf ears, but after the war, in 1946, Harker stepped in again, and this time he modified his plan with an astuteness that had marked his successful running of the Pavilion. There was no need, he said, to build a new hall; it existed already in the form of an indoor bowling green that had been

*Opposite page top:* War Days. Bomb damage to Beale's Department Store in Old Christchurch Road, Sunday, May 23rd, 1943. The Beale family has long been a part of Bournemouth life; today Nigel Beale is Chairman of the Orchestras' Management Board, and maintains a great interest in all aspects of musical activity.

*Opposite page bottom:* Getting back to normal. This photograph looking west from Bournemouth Pier was taken in 1946, and shows the wartime sea defences still in place.

The Square in 1946, note the
trolley buses. An interesting
period-point is the 90 foot spire
on St Andrews Church in Exeter
Road, removed in 1947 because
of bomb damage.

built before the war on the site of the old Glass House. Conversion
would be cheap and easy. Harker gained what probably he had
always wanted: the Pavilion would be a theatre and nothing else.
And the Bournemouth Municipal Orchestra, pulling back from what
must have seemed almost the brink of extinction, was going home
again.

# New Beginnings

Bournemouth's war damage had been – by comparison with many other towns and cities in Britain – fairly light. Nevertheless the town saw nearly 1,000 alerts, and at least two devastating air raids in 1940 and 1943, when the death toll reached 53 and 77 respectively. Thousands of properties had been damaged and nearly 250 were either completely destroyed or had to be demolished. When peace came, there was a sense of a new start, with local determination to develop amenities reflecting initially expansive plans nationwide.

The 1930's had seen great strides in public building which the war had stopped. True the old Winter Gardens, with its Victorian ambience had gone, but in its place a new red brick building had arisen. The Council had built its unique indoor bowling green at a cost of £30,000, and had opened it in November 1937. Then came the war, and the requisitioning of the place by the Air Ministry as a messing depot for the Canadian Air Force. It was not until July 1946 that it was returned to the Town, and by then Harker's master-plan had won over its council critics, and it was decided to convert it into a concert hall for the newly strengthened Bournemouth Municipal Orchestra. Furthermore, Bournemouth was to keep faith with its past and the historic site in Cranbourne Gardens: the building was to be named The Winter Gardens Concert Hall. Dan Godfrey would have been thrilled.

The next question was the problem of a musical director of the orchestra. As had been the case with Godfrey's successor, concerts were held conducted by shortlisted candidates. Montague Birch was originally among them but died shortly before the auditions began: a sad loss, although perhaps the new era really needed a new personality at the helm. Contenders for the crown were Hubert Foster Clark, Victor Fleming, John Hollingsworth, Harold Gray . . . and lastly Rudolf Schwarz. The council's musical adviser was the distinguished Mozart scholar, Edward J. Dent, but in the event, his judgement was a formality. Everyone who attended the auditions knew it had to be Schwarz from the moment his baton came down for the first time. He conducted without a score, he seemed diffident – al-

A Return to Roots. The new Winter Gardens, Bournemouth.

The interior of the new Winter Gardens in 1947. Yehudi Menuhin gives a recital before a packed house. Perhaps it was a gesture to the past to retain the occasionally placed ferns?

The Viennese School. Rudolf Schwarz in 1948

Percussionist's view. Rudolf Schwarz lifts the baton before an expectant house for a 1947 Thursday concert in the Winter Gardens.

most shy – and yet no one had heard the orchestra sound the way it did during his interpretation of Beethoven's "Eroica" symphony.

Who was this man? Austrian by birth, Rudolf Schwarz had been a former member of the Jewish Cultural Organisation in Berlin, and a prisoner in the Nazi death camp of Belsen. By October 2nd, the *Echo* reported "While workmen put the finishing touches to the interior of Bournemouth Winter Gardens in preparation for the opening concert on October 18th, the new symphony orchestra is this week having its first rehearsals under the new musical director, Rudolf Schwarz."

That opening concert brought a prolonged ovation; the concert included the Enigma Variations by Elgar, amongst other works by Wagner, Debussy and Beethoven, and the interpretion was faultless.

In the year that followed, The Winter Gardens Society was formed to support the orchestra and spread the word. One of their first – and happiest – tasks was to organise a thousand supporters to London; the Orchestra was to play at the Royal Albert Hall in October 1948 – the first time they had worked in the Metropolis since that far-off night in 1911 when Godfrey had been fêted at the Crystal Palace.

Bound for Town, 1948. Members of the Orchestra with the train chartered by the newly formed Winter Gardens Society to take supporters to London for the historic Albert Hall concert.

Rudolf Schwarz conducts the BMO at the Royal Albert Hall, London, October 24th 1948. The concert included the first performance of Malcolm Arnold's overture about London, "The Smoke" and Dvorak's G Major Symphony. The piano is set for Beethoven's C Minor Concerto, with Denis Matthews as soloist.

Cartoons by John Myers, who as Co-Principal Viola in 1949 seemed to have enough time on his hands to make these cryptic visual comments during rehearsals!

Throughout the late 'forties Schwarz – as had his forerunners – expanded the repertoire and introduced composers whose music had been neglected; Bruckner and Mahler were played to great acclaim, and Paul Tortellier played the 'Cello part in Strauss's "Don Quixote" and provoked a tumultuous reception. Beecham came and conducted the orchestra again, staying on to visit Bournemouth School for Girls, where he conducted the Bournemouth Central Schools' Orchestra during a rehearsal. The centenary of Parry fell in 1948, and the Orchestra honoured the town's famous son with a performance of his "Suite for Strings" and the inevitable "Jerusalem". As part of the 1949/50 season Kathleen Ferrier sang the contralto part in Mahler's "Das Lied von der Erde" and Schwarz – a link with the Viennese school from which the profound music sprang – drew an inspired rendition from the orchestra.

During the 1950-51 season, Schwarz announced his resignation. He had been offered a post with the City of Birmingham Symphony Orchestra, and wished to accept it. He finished the season with vivid

Beecham rehearses. After a concert with the Orchestra in 1948, Sir Thomas told the audience: "I would have to go a long way before getting better performances than I have had tonight." He was to remain a lifelong friend of the Orchestra.

55

Pierino Gamba conducts, February 1949. This fourteen-year-old boy terrorised the greatly experienced members of the BMO, but achieved incredible performances.

concerts celebrating the Festival of Britain at the new Festival Hall in London, and was for the rest of his playing career to return many times as an honoured guest.

The new Musical Director was Charles Groves. In May 1953, the Orchestra celebrated its diamond jubilee, and through that Coronation Summer, the genial, typically English Groves led the orchestra through a programme that would have pleased the founder of

1893, including a performance of Vaughan Williams' "London Symphony".

The Orchestra started to give concerts in other parts of the South and West: – at Bristol, Exeter, Plymouth, Southampton, Taunton and Truro. Furthermore, an association had begun in 1952 with the Welsh National Opera Company, and this was to prove significant in the futures of both organisations. Hugh Maguire was leader, and Groves gave youth concerts at the Winter Gardens and took over as conductor of the Municipal Choir, beginning with a version of the "Messiah" closer to anything in interpretation since the original had been heard in Handel's time.

In 1954 a new personality came on the scene who was to help shape the destiny of the Orchestra: his name was Kenneth Matchett. Matchett came to Bournemouth on a temporary basis in June of that year to assess the possibilities of the Orchestra expanding across the region. He had previously held appointments at the Liverpool Philharmonic Orchestra and the C.B.S.O. He was blunt and business-like, with a family background rooted in the music-hall tradition; he

The French 'Cellist Paul Tortelier playing the solo part in Richard Strauss's tone poem, "Don Quixote" in the 1949/50 season.

was the man for the moment – and, as it turned out, the future. He moved quickly and decisively, forming the Western Orchestral Society Ltd as an administrative force to govern orchestral affairs, funding was received from the Winter Gardens Society, the Arts Council and Bournemouth Council and the sixty strong orchestra opened the 1954/55 season with a Gala concert and a new name: The Bournemouth Symphony Orchestra. Beecham shared the conducting that night with Groves. Although it was no longer a municipally run orchestra, the BSO continued to receive support from the town of its

Orchestra and Chorus in the Winter Gardens, June 1951 for a performance of John Ireland's "These Things Shall Be". The Conductor is Schwarz and the Municipal Choir, under Chorus Master Cyril Knight, is augmented by singers from Salisbury and elsewhere, under Douglas Guest. The soloists are Sylvia Fisher, Constance Shacklock, William Herbert and William Parsons.

birth, as well as – increasingly – other centres in which it performed.

The brief to spread music throughout the region was honoured, Solomon played the "Emperor" concerto at the Winter Gardens, the links with the Welsh National Opera were strengthened, and those musicians not involved with the opera gave chamber programmes at the Winter Gardens . . . the planting of a seed that would more than ten years later grow into the Bournemouth Sinfonietta. Twice in the 1955 proms the BSO played, joined on one occasion by Myra Hess. The next season saw a new leader – Derek Collier – celebrations for

*Opposite page:* Looking towards the south-east over a web of trolleybus wires, from Commercial Road in about 1952.

Sir Arnold Bax, with the Mayor of Bournemouth and other guests at the Royal Festival Hall after a performance of his Third Symphony in 1951. The performance was critically acclaimed.

Sibelius's 90th birthday and Mozart's bi-centenary were enjoyed, and an Easter Festival once more ended the season.

In 1958 Groves received the OBE. The orchestra grew to a total of 75 players. The Municipal Choir sang at the Royal St Cecilia Concert at the Festival Hall, which also included a work by the Western Orchestral Society's President, Arthur Bliss. Mahler's centenary was celebrated in 1960 throughout the West Country with the Fourth and Fifth Symphonies, Das Lied von der Erde and the Kindertotenlieder sung by Grace Bumbry, and in the same year Groves announced his intention to resign with effect from the end of the 1960/61 season. Shortly afterwards he took up a position with the Liverpool Orchestra, but he never severed his ties with Bournemouth, returning many times to an always affectionate welcome.

The Maestro relaxes. Charles Groves at home with his wife Hilary and daughter.

Charles Groves.

February 1956:Charles Groves conducts the Bournemouth Symphony Orchestra
at the Royal Festival Hall, London.

# Stars

The Constantin Silvestri years turned the Bournemouth Symphony Orchestra into an international force. Silvestri's effect on the Orchestra has been described as being "like an electric shock", and certainly this dynamic Romanian was capable of shocking many with his sometimes controversial but always exciting interpretations. He was already a greatly admired conductor throughout Europe, and it was Kenneth Matchett's determined intention to attract just such a man in order to expand the orchestra's horizons both artistically and geographically. Silvestri's great gift was the ability to "play" the orchestra almost like a single instrument, and the result for the BSO was music-making with colours of a new intensity. His relationship with the Orchestra was that of two people who have found one another at last, and who are perfectly suited; his widow, Regina, wrote vividly of this on the occasion of the BSO's 90th anniversary:

"They loved each other deeply, married, had a lot of children – their numerous concerts – and because they were so happy together, this happiness made a beautiful sound . . . There was above all that 'something in the air' that made their performances so exciting and special, an 'extra feeling' that seemed to unite them from the very beginning, and used to bring to all their concerts the sweet magic of a 'love affair.'"

Under Silvestri a new leader – Gerald Jarvis – had been appointed, halting a run of leaders whose presence had been temporary. The deputy leader, the long-serving Alfred Jupp, had on many occasions taken the leader's chair between incumbents which numbered no less than five in a decade.

In 1965 came another 'first' – the Orchestra's television debut in Winchester Cathedral. It was on Good Friday, and they played the Prelude and Good Friday Music from Wagner's 'Parsifal'. They played at the Edinburgh Festival, the Three Choirs Festival, and in London on an increasingly regular basis, where the performances were eagerly awaited and enthusiastically received. The excitement caught on in Bournemouth too; the Winter Gardens was almost

always full when Silvestri conducted. He had star quality, and under
him the Orchestra shared star billing. Silvestri had what almost
amounted to a signature tune – Enesco's Romanian Rhapsody No.1
– and it encapsulated all the fire and sparkle of his years with the
Bournemouth orchestra.

The year 1965 was a spectacular one, and included the first
European tour, with visits to Poland, Czechoslovakia, East and West
Germany and Holland, where a critic hailed the BSO as "one of the
finest orchestras in Europe". This was followed by an emotional
event in the Winter Gardens when the Gewandhaus Orchestra under
Vaclav Neumann visited Bournemouth and were joined on the
platform by the Bournemouth string section in a huge performance
of Elgar's 'Introduction and Allegro'. 1965 also saw the centenary of

Constantin Silvestri

Silvestri with the BSO during a recording session. It has been said that Constantin Silvestri used the orchestra as his personal instrument. A London critic once said of him: "As a conductor, he is wayward, often eccentric; as an orchestral trainer he is among the world's best."

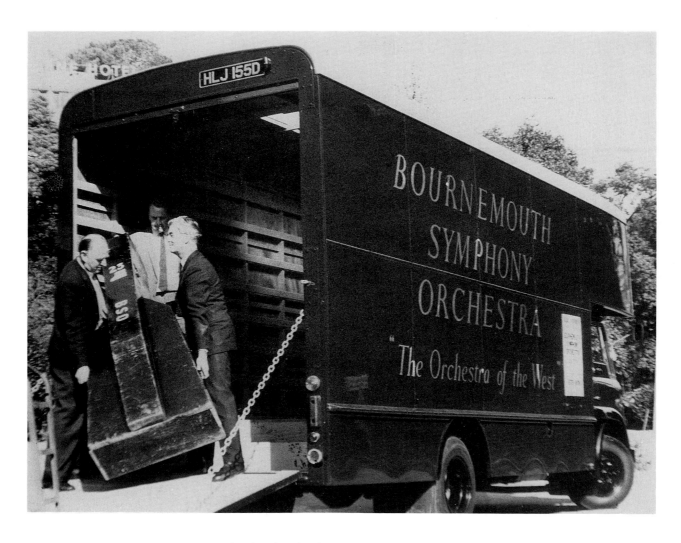

Ready for the 'Off'. The Orchestra's sense of belonging, not just to one town, but to a whole region, has been a significant factor in its survival and development. The necessary disciplines of a "travelling band" have helped to give the BSO and the Sinfonietta their distinctive characters. From the mid 1950's they have grown into a collective organisation that can justifiably and proudly call itself, "The Orchestras of the West."

the birth of Sibelius, and a taste of a future partnership when the Orchestra played under the Finnish conductor, Paavo Berglund at London's Festival Hall.

And Dan Godfrey would have been pleased to hear Silvestri's account of British music; during the sixties the Bournemouth Symphony Orchestra made what became a famous record for HMV under Silvestri of Elgar and Vaughan Williams, including "In the South", "Fantasia on a Theme of Thomas Tallis" and the Overture, "The Wasps." In everything was the same excitement – an explosive quality that anyone who was present at a Silvestri concert will never forget, but which is impossible to communicate in words. Looking back on those days from the late 1970's, the critic John J. Davis wrote:

"I was always on the edge of my seat at a Silvestri concert, never knowing quite what was going to happen. One of his tricks was to walk onto the rostrum for the last item, and if the work had a

fortissimo start, like Dvorak's "Carnival" Overture, he would whizz round and they were 'away', taking the whole audience by surprise"

More and more records appeared, giving a hint of this fire and commitment. Davis added:–

"I implore every Tchaikowsky lover to listen to the 'Italian Caprice' in Silvestri's interpretation; I've never heard a more exciting coda, which the audience in Exeter University received with wild enthusiasm in 1967."

Then in 1968 came the seventy fifth anniversary, with two successive concerts in the Royal Festival Hall, the first under Groves, the second with Silvestri, who gave a moving version of Elgar's First Symphony. In the same year came more expansion with the birth of the Bournemouth Sinfonietta. Musicians from all over the country came for the auditions, with over 70 clarinetists alone applying. In the end among the 36 musicians were a number who had moved across from the Symphony Orchestra. Indeed in those early days

Silvestri, EMI recording staff and members of the Orchestra listen to a play-back of "Scheherazade" in a studio set up in the bar of the Winter Gardens, 1966. The unrivalled acoustic of the Winter Gardens made it an ideal place for orchestral recording. Following an earlier broadcast, Desmond Shawe-Taylor wrote in the Sunday Times:"The string choir plays with a fulness and warmth which are rare in England; the woodwind is clear, firm and accurate; and the brass is superb."

Musicians together, 1965. During a tour of Britain by the Leipzig Gewandhaus Orchestra under Vaclav Neumann, the string sections of the two orchestras joined forces on stage at the Winter Gardens in a performance of Elgar's "Introduction and Allegro", and afterwards, more informally, at a party. On both occasions, music-making inevitably was the number-one priority!

The 75th Anniversary Dinner, held in the Pavilion, Bournemouth. The diminutive figure of Constantin Silvestri stands before a portrait of Sir Dan Godfrey. Sir Alan Cobham, the aviation pioneer, first Chairman of the Western Orchestral Society stands on the extreme left, with Sir John Eden on the extreme right, next to Madame Silvestri and Sir Michael Tippett.

musicians moved between both orchestras, and had to consult a weekly chart in order to see who they were with and where and what they were playing! The idea did not last long . . . to the relief of most people involved!

The first Sinfonietta concerts were given in Ringwood, Wimborne and Christchurch under George Hurst and Assistant Conductor Nicholas Braithwaite. Shortly after this came the first West of England tour. The seed had been planted years before, and the need for a smaller orchestra to play at venues throughout the South and West had grown more pressing; yet the Sinfonietta quickly established itself as a major force in its own right under conductors such as George Hurst, Kenneth Montgomery and Wolker Wangenheim. The orchestra achieved – and has kept – its own distinctive personality. Meanwhile the parent orchestra gained a new leader, Brendan O'Brien.

The sixties were heady, almost breathless times for West Country music. For Constantin Silvestri, the fire went out in February 1969. He had been ailing for several months, and on the day before he died, his place had been taken on the Festival Hall rostrum by the Czech conductor, Zdenek Macal, with Paul Tortellier playing the

Shirt-sleeve Symphony. Rudolf Schwarz rehearses in 1971. Until the move to Poole the Orchestra made use of various rehearsal venues, including Bournemouth School for Girls and Trinity Hall in Old Christchurch Road. Schwarz continued his association with the Orchestra after his post-war years as Musical Director, and frequently returned as guest conductor until his retirement.

George Hurst and Radu Lupu
backstage at the Colston Hall
Bristol on June 6th, 1973, before
a concert in aid of the Basle Air
Disaster Fund. After Silvestri's
death in 1969, Hurst took over
responsibility for many of the
concerts under the title of Artistic
Adviser, bridging the gap until
the appointment of Paavo
Berglund. He was to remain a
long-term stalwart friend of the
BSO.

'Cello solo in Strauss's 'Don Quixote'. Those who were there felt the
spirit of Silvestri in the orchestra's playing that night, and then the
next day brought the news of his death. He was fifty five.

Seldom has a musician been more greatly mourned and more sadly
missed. The 'Silvestri years' are still spoken of with a kind of awe by
musicians and concert-goers alike; he had loved Bournemouth, and
was buried in the rich soil of St Peter's Church, close to the grave of
Dan Godfrey. At the funeral the whole orchestra was present. The
memorial concert – conducted by Rudolf Schwarz at Silvestri's re-
quest – was Mahler's Seventh Symphony, which they played in Exeter, Bristol and Bournemouth. The Orchestra's administration offices contain a bronze relief memorial to Silvestri.

Finding a successor to such a man was not easy; Matchett and his
board did not rush into a quick decision, but George Hurst, already
associated with both orchestras, was given the title "Artistic Adviser" and became in effect Principal Conductor at the same time. In
1970, Kenneth Montgomery became his assistant, and a year later

Maurice Gendron was appointed as Conductor/Director of the Sinfonietta. There were guest conductors too – and continuing innovation, including the World Premiere of Jonathan Harvey's complex and thrilling blend of orchestral and electronic sound in his 'Cantata VII, On Vision'. This was given at Southampton Guildhall under Peter Evans, the University's Professor of Music.

Then in 1972, the orchestra found its new Principal Conductor; Paavo Berglund, who had conducted the BSO during the Sibelius centenary, now took over at the rostrum. He was as different from Silvestri as it was possible to be. Where the Romanian's music had been hot and colourful, the Fin's was dark and cool. Berglund was a native of Helsinki, and had begun his career as a violinist with the Finnish Radio Orchestra, in time becoming its conductor. He had met Sibelius, and was acknowledged as one of his principal interpreters.

His days with the BSO began in spectacular fashion with the world premiere recording of Sibelius' Kullervo Symphony. This prefaced

Paavo Berglund, who became Principal Conductor, Bournemouth Symphony Orchestra in 1972.

73

Paavo Berglund with the Orchestra on Southern Television.

an intensive recording programme through the 1970's, during which the orchestra under Berglund recorded all the Sibelius symphonies, as well as the Violin concerto with Ida Haendel. Also with Berglund the BSO became noted for their Shostakovich interpretations. For many members of the orchestra, the high point of the Berglund years came with a tour of Finland in 1976, during which time they played at the Helsinki Festival, as well as in the most northerly concert hall in the world. They also played in Russia.

The 1970's had been busy and productive years in other ways; in the year Berglund joined the BSO, the Sinfonietta Choir had been formed. In 1973 Kenneth Montgomery became principal conductor of the Sinfonietta. The following year saw Kenneth Matchett signing an exclusive recording contract with EMI, and the John Player International Conductor's Award, won by Simon Rattle, who, for his prize, gained a two year contract to conduct the orchestras. He was also to make a spectacular recording of Mahler's unfinished Tenth Symphony for EMI before the City of Birmingham Symphony Orchestra claimed him. In 1975 Edward Heath conducted the BSO at a Gala concert in the Pavilion. 1977 saw Kenneth Montgomery vacate his Sinfonietta post to take up an appointment in Holland, and his place was taken by Wolker Wangenheim.

74

# Upward and On

In 1978 the BSO played ten concerts at the Hong Kong Festival under Berglund. Also in attendance were soprano Felicity Palmer and pianist Peter Frankl. Meanwhile at home in the same year, a major and exciting new arts and entertainment venue opened opposite the Bus station and Arndale shopping centre in Poole. Poole Arts Centre was designed to provide every facility under one roof: a theatre, art and exhibition studios, dance studios ... and a well-appointed concert hall, The Wessex Hall. Also built into the structure were a number of floors of office space, and in 1979, the Western Orchestral Society moved its administrative base here from Gervis Place. At around the same time, changes were going on within the choir. Up until now it had retained a link with the past in its title of The Bournemouth Municipal Choir. Now it was brought into line with the developments of recent years, becoming part of the Western Orchestral Society, and being renamed as The Bournemouth Symphony Chorus.

Meanwhile, Kenneth Matchett was succeeded by Keith Whitmore as General Administrator. At about the same time a new supportive group for the Orchestras was formed in the Friends of the Bournemouth Orchestras. The Friends were to play a major part in preserving the musical heritage of the South West, with groups springing up throughout the region: in Bridport, Bristol, Exeter, Southampton, Portsmouth, Yeovil and Weymouth as well as in Bournemouth and Poole. In the midst of all this, the BSO gained a new Principal Conductor, a young Israeli, Uri Segal, while Ronald Thomas was appointed as Musical Director the Sinfonietta.

In the Spring of 1981 the BSO toured Switzerland, Austria and West Germany. Then, in July, came one of the most memorable events in the Orchestra's latter-day history, when they were reunited with their former Principal Conductor, Paavo Berglund, to play a Sibelius cycle at the Savonlinna Opera Festival in Finland. Berglund – never a man for extravagant words – remembered the occasion vividly:

"Especially I remember the tour in 1981 to Savonlinna, where the

*Following page*: Taking a Bow. The Bournemouth Sinfonietta and Ronald Thomas acknowledge applause at London's Queen Elizabeth Hall. Thomas was appointed as Musical Director of the Sinfonietta in 1980

Royal Visit to Poole, March 23rd, 1979. Long-serving BSO member David Sheen is presented to the Queen during a rehearsal before an invited audience in the Wessex Hall of Poole Arts Centre. Prince Philip meanwhile chats to other members of the Orchestra.

BSO's concerts were unanimously praised as the highlight of the Opera Festival. Personally I think these Sibelius concerts in Finland have been among the best concerts that I ever have conducted."

Meanwhile, the Sinfonietta, its reputation as a virtuoso ensemble growing almost daily, raised the Bournemouth Orchestral standard again in Switzerland, with an appearance under Edward Heath at Davos. And as if to place a positive seal on what was seen by many as a new start for the Orchestras, Madame Silvestri unveiled the memorial to her husband at the W.O.S. offices in Poole.

The 1980's were exciting times for the Western Orchestral Society, and in 1983, a new Chief Executive, David Richardson, took over the helm. The BSO was in its 90th year, it had a new and distinguished conductor, Rudolf Barshai, who promised to do for Shostakovich what Berglund had done for Sibelius in the West of England. And by now there could be no doubt that the Bournemouth Symphony Orchestra and Bournemouth Sinfonietta were truly "The Orchestras of the West".

Meanwhile the Bournemouth Sinfonietta had been enhancing its reputation through work with Glyndebourne Touring Opera. This association ended in 1986, but it heralded a new era for the orchestra. Roger Norrington became its Principal Conductor, and its recording schedule – with its reputation as a first-class chamber orchestra – increased. It was also freer now to develop its educational and community work, a field that may prove to be a significant part of the future of orchestral music. Under the guidance of Education Officer Michael Henson, members of the Sinfonietta went into schools throughout the region, including the Scilly Isles, giving workshops and lunchtime concerts, and inviting amateur musicians to join them for al fresco performances.

These educational initiatives were emulated by the Symphony Or-

Uri Segal. Appointed Principal Conductor, BSO in 1980, Segal, born in Jerusalem in 1944, spent only two seasons with the Bournemouth Symphony Orchestra as Principal Conductor, but during that time gave a number of memorable performances, including Mahler's 2nd Symphony at the Winter Gardens, and a remarkable recording of Britten's Symphonic Suite, "Gloriana" and the same composer's only work directly written for the ballet, "The Prince of the Pagodas."

*Right:* Norman Del Mar. A long-term friend of the Orchestras, who was appointed Principal Guest Conductor of the Sinfonietta in 1982. A man after Dan Godfrey's heart, he achieved an international reputation, while remaining typically English.

*Below:* BSO & DYO. Conductor Owain Arwel Hughes takes a bow with the Bournemouth Symphony Orchestra and the Dorset Youth Orchestra after a successful Prom concert at Poole's Wessex Hall.

Rudolf Barshai conducts. Appointed Principal Conductor, BSO in 1982, the Russian-born Barshai, who was a pupil of Dmitri Shostakovitch, brought an intimate knowledge of contemporary Russian masters to his time as Principal Conductor. After a highly successful period as a solo viola player with an international reputation, he founded the Moscow Chamber Orchestra in 1955. His distinguished career has included work with such legendary names as Gilels, Richter, Oistrakh and Rostropovich.

81

Music in Camera. The Symphony Orchestra on TVS, conducted by Christopher Seaman.

chestra as it staged a series of Family and Children's concerts at the Winter Gardens, Bournemouth. The "Mega Music Shows" as they became known, had explored the role of the sponsor – in this case Bournemouth's *Evening Echo* – as a practical participant in the concert-giving process. Harvey's of Bristol had already showed the way in sponsorship both for concerts and for records, and others followed suit, including Bournemouth's Commercial Radio Station, 2CR, who sponsored a performance of Mahler's Second Symphony in the Winter Gardens during the early 1980's.

In 1987, The Bournemouth Symphony Orchestra announced the appointment of a new Principal Conductor, a man who had already joined the Orchestra as principal guest conductor. His name was Andrew Litton, and his role was to be rather different to some of the foregoing incumbents of his post. He was, in effect, to be closer to

82

the position Dan Godfrey had occupied, that is, as music director, with a hand in the artistic planning of seasons, as well as being a crucially public part of their execution.

It appeared to be – from the very first – one of those love affairs between conductor and orchestra that occasionally happens, and which has happened on a number of occasions to the Bournemouth Orchestras. Litton summed it up on the occasion of his appointment:

"There was an immediate sort of chemistry which I have since grown very spoiled by. I find it on very few occasions, and I have been told that I will by others who are much more experienced. Everyone on the platform there has the same desires as I do to make the most of each moment."

Litton took his orchestra to the Proms at the Royal Albert Hall in 1990, and made records with them of Tchaikowsky Symphonies, as

Record Breakers! Members of Bournemouth Sinfonietta at BBC Television Centre in London, where they broke the world record for the most number of people playing a double bass at one time. The record they set was 18 people. The feat was achieved as part of BBC1's Recordbreakers programme, and the musicians also played the programme's signature tune, "Dedication" in an arrangement by Carl Davis (Bottom left.) Also in the picture are the programme's presenters, Cheryl Baker (Left) and Roy Castle (Suspended, right.)

well as works by Franck, Leonard Bernstein, Gershwin and Ravel, often with Litton as soloist as well as conductor.

Litton's appointment to the Symphony Orchestra was followed by that of the distinguished Hungarian-born pianist and conductor Tamas Vasary to the Sinfonietta, following an acclaimed tour of Germany in 1987 which included concerts in Leipzig and Berlin. Vasary has subsequently shared the development of the Orchestra with the Director and Associate Conductor of the Bournemouth Sinfonietta, Richard Studt. Under them, the recording career of the Sinfonietta has also burgeoned, with discs by Martinu, Honegger and Richard Strauss among many others.

1991, the year the Bournemouth Orchestras welcomed a new Managing Director in Anthony Woodcock, saw the start of a bold new arts initiative in Bournemouth with the birth of the Bournemouth International Festival; not just a music festival, as in bygone days, but a feast of the arts in all its varied forms. And appropriately, there were the BSO and the Sinfonietta at the heart of the celebrations, where else, but at the Winter Gardens? In 1992 the event was developed, and the orchestras' involvement consolidated.

During July, the BSO staged three spectacular open-air concerts in Bournemouth's Meyrick Park, on a specially constructed floodlit stage. The opening night, as if in tribute to the Dan Godfrey tradition, ended with the 1812 Overture, complete with cannon and mortar effects. As 1992 moved towards its autumn the Poole Proms – now a major part of the Orchestras' latter-day lives – began; six concerts in eight days including an evening devoted to the music of Walt Disney's 'Fantasia', a programme of orchestral arrangements of themes from Andrew Lloyd Webber's best-loved musicals, and a traditional 'last night of the Proms'. There was one cloud over the year, when Sir Charles Groves, such a friend for so long, died.

The 1992/93 season, full of the variety that has made the Orchestras so belovedly unpredictable, was opened by the BSO's new Principal Guest Conductor, Richard Hickox, with a concert that included – perhaps symbolically – an English work by a major living composer . . . a man who also happened to be the President of the organisation that runs the BSO and Sinfonietta, Michael Tippett. Later in the season came Vaughan Williams – his Third Symphony – amidst the Beethoven, Tchaikowsky and Wagner. Dan Godfrey would have been pleased. The opening weeks of the season also included a concert of Mahler and Beethoven conducted by the Orchestra's Chief Guest Conductor, Kees Bakels, who established himself quickly as an important part of the artistic team. Meanwhile the Sinfonietta – in addition to its other commitments throughout the region – held a Winter residency at Weymouth Pavilion under

84

Tamas Vasary, who directed the Orchestra from the keyboard in concertos by Beethoven, Chopin and Mozart.

The world of the Bournemouth Orchestras will always be a changing one. A 1994 tour of the USA, a vibrant concert-giving programme ever-aware of commercial requirements, and an increasing commitment to community and educational projects bear witness to that. But it is fitting that for its centenary concert in May 1993, the Bournemouth Symphony Orchestra should have come home to the Winter Gardens, Bournemouth. For Bournemouth must always be remembered as the first place ever to support and run a permanent municipal orchestra. It is right that the great musical force that has grown out of Sir Dan's group of musicians amongst the potted palms in the old 'Glass House', should today carry the name of Bournemouth around the world.

And it is also fitting that for that centenary, the BSO should have chosen a giant celebration enfolding the Symphony Orchestra and Chorus:– Mahler's Second Symphony – "The Resurrection Symphony" ending with a final triumphant poem carrying an eternal sentiment that – in the emotion of the moment – might well be taken as a statement of a hundred years of musical achievement:

"O believe, my heart, O believe,
    nothing of you will be lost!
What you longed for is yours,
    yours what you loved,
What you championed!"

*Right:* Music and Science Workshop. Cellist Janet Sim working with pupils at one of the growing number of educational workshops.

*Below*: The Mega Music Show. A critical member of the audience studies the technical prowess of BSO Bass Clarinetist Norman Hallam at one of the popular Winter Gardens children's concerts, sponsored by the *Evening Echo*.

*Above:* The Bournemouth
Symphony Chorus. The Chorus
have often found themselves at
the cutting edge of contemporary
music-making. At their very first
appearance – on Tuesday, 14th
November 1911, they gave two
performances of Edward
German's "Merrie England",
with the composer conducting –
in one day. Here they are seen
rehearsing David Fanshawe's
"African Sanctus" with Owain
Arwel Hughes.

*Left:* Tamas Vasary. A fine study
in concentration: the
distinguished Hungarian-born
pianist and conductor in action
with the Bournemouth
Sinfonietta.

Behind the Scenes. Orchestra members prepare to take the stage at the Royal
Festival Hall, London.

Brendan O'Brien, Leader, Bournemouth Symphony Orchestra.

Richard Studt, director and Associate Conductor, Bournemouth Sinfonietta.
Playing his 1724 Stradivarius known as 'The Dolphus'. Studt frequently directs
the Sinfonietta, as well as other chamber orchestras, including the London
Virtuosi, the Concertante of London and his own ensemble, the Tate Music
Group of London.

BSO Principal Flute, Karen Jones
shares a joke with former Prime
Minister Edward Heath.

Time Out for Trombones. The
brass section relaxes during a
rehearsal.

Richard Hickox. In September 1992, Richard Hickox conducted the opening concert of the 92/93 season in his new capacity as Principal Guest Conductor. Appropriately for a musician well known for his affinity with the music of British composers, Hickox began the season with a performance of the 4th Symphony by Michael Tippett, the Bournemouth Orchestras' President Emeritus. He was at the same time involved in a project to record all of Tippett's orchestral works with the BSO.

Kees Bakels. Bakels became Chief Guest Conductor of the BSO in 1992 after a number of years when he developed a close relationship with the Orchestra. Born in Amsterdam, he began his career as a violinist. He is also a noted interpreter of Opera. Bakels has a catholic taste in programme building, and takes an increasing interest in English music.

*Above:* The Bournemouth Symphony Orchestra on the steps of the Portsmouth Guildhall.

*Opposite page:* Andrew Litton, Principal Conductor and Artistic Adviser, Bournemouth Symphony Orchestra. He came to international attention in 1982, while still a pupil at the Julliard School, as the first American and youngest winner of the London BBC International Conductors Competition. He took up his Bournemouth post in 1988. Under his baton, the Bournemouth Symphony Orchestra has increased its standing, and has a justifiable reputation as one of the finest orchestras in the country.